# Small Favors

# Small Favors

Poems by

Diane Stone

Cover design by Shay Culligan

ISBN: 978-1-952326-78-3

Kelsay Books
502 South 1040 East, A-119
American Fork, Utah, 84003

For Greg, whose gardens inspire

# Acknowledgments

*Bacopa Literary Review* (Writers Alliance of Gainesville): "Local Weather," First Place in 2015 Annual Poetry Contest

*Cascade* (Washington Poets Association): "Celebration"

*Coffee Poems* (World Enough Writers): "How to Fell an Alder"

*Embers and Flames* (Outrider Press): "Mourning a Tanager"

*5 A.M.:* "Buddhas in the Pasture"

*Floating Bridge Review* (Floating Bridge Press): "Spring Mowing"

*Free Lunch:* "Dog Days"

*Her Mark Datebook* (Woman Made Gallery): "Local Concerns"

*Jewish Currents—World to Come:* "What the Earth Knows"

*Last Call: The Anthology of Beer, Wine, & Spirits Poetry* (World Enough Writers): "Revelry," "Summer Solstice, Double Bluff"

*Main Channel Voices:* "Coyote Kill"

*Minerva Rising:* "Harvest," "Say Yes"

*Rattle:* "Why Men Go Crabbing"; reprinted in *Pontoon* (Floating Bridge Press)

*Soundings Review:* "The Cat's Grave"

*The Comstock Review:* "Making Applesauce"

*The Main Street Rag:* "Our Closest Neighbor"

*Third Wednesday:* "The Bright Side"

*Through a Distant Lens* (Write Wing Publishing): "Last Night's Chicken Curry"

*Windfall:* "Ordinary"

*Your Daily Poem:* "Changing"


With special thanks to mentor and poet Stellasue Lee and to poets Sheryl Clough and Lois Edstrom for their ongoing support and friendship.

# Contents

# Our Private Fields

I say to my husband, "I'm worried
about this world—hunger, climate change.
What the heck's going on?"
He raises a stiff hand, calloused from all-season work.
"Not now," he says, "too many chores: blades to sharpen,
fields to mow before wet weather closes summer down."

Days later, I say, "So what about this world—
polluted air, needless wars, wolves getting shot?
I'm sick of it."
He looks at me: "Later, okay?"
He's got cover crops to plant and wood chips
to blanket those bald spots on the slope
where blackberry canes thick as his wrist dulled
those very blades he newly sharpened.

Soon as I'd stopped fretting about the world situation,
he says, "What's that about wolves and war?"
But now I'm busy kneading bread, and I have a story
in my head for the grandkids about Stanley Starfish.
Fava beans are ready to blanch and freeze;
corn's tasseled, waiting for me or that raccoon
homesteading on our choicest acre.

That's how it is around here:
sweet dailiness, our drug of choice.
Are they wrong, these guilty pleasures,
the joys abiding in our private fields?

# The Bright Side

Some headlines are enough
to make you weep—
tigers scratching at the brink,

plastics and more plastics
gumming up the works,
forests slashed to stumps,

ample floods for a second ark.
*Homo ignoramus,* I presume.
Yet the Earth chugs on.

November's leaves dropped on cue,
so something's going right.
Big yellow leaves, small red ones

sway through a haze
of morning drizzle.
They dropped all day

nudged by a slight breeze:
tawny little parachutes,
orange tatters of summer
easing down to a damp, soft rot.

# Say Yes

After too many seasons of no
and maybe, I've signed on to yes.
No to this, no to that—forget it.
Earth spins in its yes alignment,
moon and stars just so.
I won't curse weeds
or the neighbor's yappy dog
or that banshee chainsaw
splintering trees.
No hysterics, I promise,
when storms shut off the lights;
no screams at mouse turds
sowed like oiled seeds
in the downstairs bath.

While Prince Kitty sleeps
on a sun-drenched ledge,
his mighty tail curled
in yes contentment,
I remind myself: yes to fur,
yes to heat and dusty summer.
Yes even to rain and cancelled parades.
Yes to that spotted jewel
of a ladybug whose dainty feet
prowl my kitchen counter.
Apples nap in a willow basket—
yes to the honeyed scent,
yes to the flesh, yes even to the bruises.

# How to Fell an Alder

First you need a spouse
to tell you not to do it.
But of course you must do it.
That old tree drops dead wood
on the main path to the barn—
sways above the wood shed,
reminds you of tasks
you didn't finish or even start.

You make a pot of coffee
and review the whole plan:
extension ladder, pruning saw,
steel cable, old Sears chainsaw
to oil, coddle, crank.

The tree stands tall, green
and leafy, an honest soldier.
In that moment between felling
and not felling, resolve shifts
as if your own deep roots
have lost their grip. You feel
too much a part of these woods
to add one more slash
of destruction.
Take a deep breath.

When the tree crashes down
just where you planned it,
triumph isn't what you feel;
regret maybe, even remorse.

# Small Favors

Last night I slept a good eight hours,
not once panicked by a heart
bulging like a briefcase of troubles.
I survived midnight's indigestion,
dozed through a B-string of nightmares
all exploiting my most recent regrets.

This morning's toast popped up crisp
on both sides, just the way I like it,
and my coffee was strong enough
to boot me out the door.
Neighbors, even the surly one,
waved as we rejoiced
at the benevolence of blue skies.
At the grocery store, I beat the crowds;
empty parking spaces beckoned,
carts rolled in my direction.

After dinner, my tea bag didn't slip
from its staple; the cream tasted sweet.
As night enclosed me like a flannel sleeve,
I settled in, content, no bleating sheep
lined up for mandatory counting.
All seemed well in the kingdom of now.
Some days are magical,
the way small favors settle into place.

# Our Closest Neighbor

He shoots rabbits for fun. And coyotes too.
To him, deer are just big rats. And he hates rats.
He's got no use for tree-huggers and cry babies
out to save yesterday's world. Survival is his frame
of reference; it's him against the do-gooders.
In summer he straps a torpedo on his back
to eradicate weeds and anything else in his path.
His home is his fortress.

Yet he helped clear our ditch, working for hours
knee deep in muck. When he and I pass on the road,
we talk about rain and the community well, exchange
tips on digging potatoes. He's our closest neighbor,
but each of us knows the difference between neighbor
and friend.

# Making Applesauce

Each harvest could be our last,
so don't waste time looking for perfection.
Forget the reddest, the biggest;
be happy with any ripe ones,
especially those that call your name
from inside their dark, full clutch of seed.
Only today is perfect, clear and sunny.
In this quiet room beneath the canopy
of leaves and red confusion,
apples hang in perfect patterns,
like promises kept:
the trees to us, us to the fruit.

Bite the first one with your eyes closed.
Toss the second to the edge of the woods;
later, the doe will find it.
Be small, unbusy as a bee folding its wings
in the empty nest of summer's end.
Tell that clerk in charge of your mind to relax.
And the priest counting orbits of doubts
in your soul, please, put him to sleep at the wheel.
Your eyes and hands are devotion enough.

Recipes don't matter, just the steady work
of peel, core, slice, simmer.
At last, the buzzing mind settles
in its saucer of cream and plenty.

# Spring Mowing

This spring we set the blades higher,
and then higher still,
to avoid nests
and drowsy snakes
tucked among tall grasses.

But not high enough.
A perfect nest, cupped and warm,
tumbles to the edge of my swath,
and five spotted eggs scatter among stubble
as a yellow bird flutters in the tractor's wake.

No matter that I deliver the nest
and unscathed eggs to safer grass,
I can't undo what's done.
After each loss, silence settles
with a mocking calm.
But this lull in deeds is brief,
and soon the old quickening begins.

# Mourning a Tanager

Last week I found a tanager,
its orange-gold body stiff
but vivid in the grass.

In less than three days,
its flame dwindled
to an untidy heap
of ash and disjointed bones,
few signs of the living bird
splashing color in the bath.

Ants claimed its pale remains,
marching through blind eye sockets,
in and out of rigid claws,
across a mandible intact but mute.

When I spotted two evening grosbeaks
feeding near the pond, I moved
in their direction, enticed by flashes
of yellow, black, and white.
Such a fickle mourner I am,
easily swerving to brighter flames.

# What the Earth Knows

Don't rush to dig or weed.
First map your land's quirks:
its parched shoulders, secret bends,
the crevices where rain collects.
Turn your back on exotic flowers
and let your fields go native.
They'll rejoice and so will you
at the wind-dance
of red fescue's panicles nodding
in the same warm direction.
Be braver than you've been so far.
Conjure bogs. Welcome raptors.
Treat dirt as if the world deserves a future.

Each spring scatter a few hundred seeds;
wind will push the faithful ones back home.
Leave them where they land;
they know more than you
about designs and patterns;
how in the beginning,
beauty might seem a mistake
caught in a clutch of thin stems
and pinched leaves.
Months later, you look again,
transfixed, and find a masterpiece.

# Ordinary

Nothing much happened today.
The sun trotted west,
same as always, looking for thrills
but finding the same far-off horizon.
That sky-high cedar near the porch
stayed rooted to the same ferny spot;
it's been there a hundred years at least.
The same black-headed grosbeak splashed
in the same stone fountain
then fluttered dry on a stalk.

In the field, a chugging tractor
rattled the walls of this clear afternoon.
Our mutt, startled by the commotion,
heckled the neighbor's chickens,
who clucked head-first across the road.
A nice guy braked: no dead chickens,
no bickering about right of way
or who got there first.

Nothing much happened in the garden either.
Corn didn't sprout but thought about it;
thistles in purple caps bunched
like kids against the fence line,
waiting for a chance to sprint.
As usual, the mailman honked twice
and waved. We waved back.

If we can manage a day like this one—
no tanks or feuds uprooting corn,
no cedars trashed for dollars of despair,
no bad blood spilt among neighbors or chickens—
maybe we can do the same tomorrow
and the day after that,
and at last say to our children
(who think we're dopes
and honestly who can blame them),
See. There's hope, and time enough
to do the heart's real work.

# Rich

We're rich, I tell him,
plenty rich despite the odds:
ripe berries for breakfast,
sunrise burning off last night's fog.
Sure, the south corner's swampy,
but who cares?
Mallards nest in the damp scape of sedge,
and blackbirds dip like balance toys
on cattails and reeds, flashing
scarlet patches at the bees.
The mutt that howled five weeks straight
finally made friends with the cat.
So rich, this quiet.

We've got quilts on the bed,
few grudges in our pockets.
I know the barn roof leaks
along a zigzag of buckets,
but the shop's dry enough.
Even when the old truck's slow to start,
we can sweet-talk it if we want.
Thistles mug the orchard,
and the garden fence derailed,
but we've got joy stashed
in more than one account.

This morning a doe stood by the gate,
blessing our garden with her eyes.

## Coyote Kill

We heard a kill last night.
Coyotes down the road
in a neighbor's field
caught a spring calf
or maybe the fawn
we doted on all summer,
hoping it might live the season.
I hope they didn't kill that fawn.

There was yipping, yapping,
barking, growling,
as if something immense
had grabbed the empty space
we take for granted—
our cup of world flipped upside down.

I pictured coyotes in gleaming fur,
paws damp with blood,
charmed fangs doing what they must.
Excited pups pranced
beside the almost corpse
whose hooves still thrashed.
Howls turned to whimpers,
whimpers to shrill, sing-song yelps.

Quick as it started, a blessed quiet.
That sudden quiet was louder than the kill.

# Taking the Back Roads

Before the interstates
metastasized across America,
we drove down narrow roads
patched with tar, our barge-like cars
pushing through plantation pines
with scrub oak and palmettos
scrabbling at the edges,
while insects smacked
against the windshield.

I still take the back roads,
driving sweet two lanes
in a sound-world of tread
that uncoils in gentle hums
through soil-bound towns
where people make do
on the outskirts and tend tired plots,
people who raise hens and bees,
who toil with hoes and rakes
rough in their palms,
honey and jam for sale roadside.
When I pass, they wave.

# Another Day at the Beach

As gulls sail through the blurry haze
and light rain nips my chilled face,

a guy nearby opens the back of his truck
and releases a dozen racing pigeons.

Gray and white, they flash from his truck
more light than bird. They wheel

above the sea in the shape of a Z,
silver glints arrowing the rain,

back and forth, quick, bright,
and then disappear south.

They'll get home before me,
he says, revving his engine.

# Why Men Go Crabbing

Something about men and boats:
the hopeful way they nod
to each other, even
before the wind kicks up
and grants permission.

The honest way men clamber
over gunwales, hauling bum knees,
muscles stiff from wading
through cold waves
with traps and oars in hand,
out of breath and out of shape
yet willing to lend tired arms to pain.

They know the rules of daily limits
and closed waters, the art of knots
and bait buckets packed
with expectations.
But joy is something else,
something more than reading tides
and steering clear of shoals;
it's more about—*somehow*—
getting one damn thing just right.

# Local Concerns

1

Next time you see that five-point buck,
notice his left eye—it looks blind to me,
oyster-gray and blank.
He hangs out with the yearling doe,
the little scruffy one who bellies
under the hog wire to steal our berries.


2

Alert to Neighbors:
The new owners of the Quinnell land
plan to log it—those nine acres
of second-growth across from Ruth's pond.
Let's meet at my place tonight, 7:30.
Ruth says don't tell Ralph about the logging.
He's sick enough already;
more stress will likely kill him.
Chuck, please don't bring your dogs.
Our cat goes berserk.


3

What about that snapped hemlock—
firewood or snag?
The birds are giving it a workout.
Three kinds of woodpeckers drill the bark,
and those little gray-suited guys
with stumpy tails slide down headfirst.
Yesterday a red tail perched there until the sun dropped.
On second thought, we've got plenty wood for now.

# The Cat's Grave

Coyotes can sniff death two feet under,
so I dig deeper than that,
down to the scrape of hardpan.
Digging a grave is hard enough
without these rocks blocking
the sorrow work of shovels.
When his grave's an honest fit,
smooth and rock free,
I lower him in it,
his curved shape
bundled in a torn green towel.

Something's missing.
Maybe it's the dumb face
of his devotion.
For him I was god-like,
performing the daily rituals
of open doors and treats.
Now I'm mortal again,
without my one true believer.
Here's my last wish:
that he sleep the long nap of honest rot
with no moonlit claws scratching at the surface.
The least I can do is dig deep enough,
more than two feet under.

# Hog Heaven

It's that scatter of half-light
near the pond, where
I gather my thoughts
at the end of the day—
no fireworks or epiphanies,
just the sun sliding down
its usual escape and
a disgruntled heron
expecting a private pond.

It's where Grandpa snoozes
on the sofa after Sunday dinner
with his old cat perched
on the prow of his chest
like a helmsman, ready to steer
their dreams in a happy direction.

It's where perfect biscuits rise
with encores of flavor,
where night-blooming jasmines
sweeten frog-filled nights.

It's that slow afternoon
when the kid down the road
brings me a dozen fresh eggs
and describes the love life
of his chickens
and what broody means.

# Buddhas in the Pasture

Of all the animals, most blessed are cows;
the way they lean serenely on their shadows,
breathing light, soft eyes herding
blades of grass between their hooves.
Every spring the calves arrive,
wide-eyed and bawling, until they
evolve like gangly saints
into their noble, grown-up selves.

Cows ask so little from us humans—
not that we love them or amuse them;
not even that we recall briefly, after dinner,
the serial nods of heavy heads,
the architecture of four agile stomachs
transforming grass to cud, ever so discreetly.

Wrapped in the supple hide of cowness,
they shuffle forward, nose to haunch.
As they plod green fields,
their simple souls rise up and up
like bright balloons that hover
well above the suffering of pastures.

# Harvest

Here's a seed
tipped in the slight trench
of a long, straight row;
and the row itself slightly tipped,
aligned along the parallels
of taut string lashed to cedar stakes,
loose straw shuffled
in aisles of damp earth.
And here are gifts from air:
not just seeds or starts
but light and time,
rain and glazed nights,
even the spark of words;
all these, believable and believed in.

It's true,
we're least among the miracles.
Forget prayers;
heat spins the timeless wheel,
turns the soil,
unzips the seed
from its winter suit,
pries sap from brute sleep.
Right now we're breathless from the heat,
dizzy as we labor on our knees,
imagining the feast.

# Refuge

First I call Kin and Ginny:
Come Friday night—we're having a feast.
At the beach, I pick my limit of clams
in less than twenty minutes
and do it two days straight.

Greg harvests kale, chard, beans,
squash, and three kinds of lettuce.
Friday we cook like crazy:
clams in wine and butter sauce,
hard-crusted bread, grilled squash,
salad so fresh it whistles,
raspberry pie bubbly in the center.

We aren't religious people,
but when we gather at our table
with friends and good food,
we feel like ancient congregants
huddled in a fire-lit cave, safe for now:
inside, a refuge for feast and tribe;
outside, troubling signs from the sky
and odd beasts loose on the prairies.

# Summer Solstice, Double Bluff

It's a wonder we care anymore,
knowing what we know about reversals,
changes of heart, second chances
hanging by a thread.
Watch out, kids; here comes fate
barreling down the drive,
brake fluid low, a distracted god
snoozing at the wheel.

There's more bad news:
some wrens have changed their tunes,
and whales are starving in a sea of plastic garbage.
Golden paintbrush waves goodbye
from the deck of a waning palette.
We might be next, from what I read.

We gather on the beach
with glasses of champagne
to toast this longest light
even if dark nods just around the bend.
The longest day's no sooner here
than it bails out too,
leaving us stranded
with our towels and doubts,
gulls grieving overhead.

As we lay on our backs
beneath a carousel sky,
frowns soften, fists unclench.
What a spectacle we are—
slowly spinning on this crazy wheel
called now and tomorrow and all at once.

# Dog Days

We don't discuss big issues now, not in this heat.
Not last year's World Series or climate change,
no words whittled into daggers of contention.
The most we can muster is small talk
about cleaning crab and who wants a beer.
The sun plods headlong down its pike,
leaving us in a slump of small intentions.
Mom's ashes snooze in their jar,
content, I think, considering her predicament.
As a neighbor remarked,
It's a straight shot to paradise from here.

Then the quail's three-note rant
(Chi-**ca**-go, Chi-**ca**-go)
draws us to the warm side of the porch.
As if that's not enough for one summer day,
the mail arrives early, along with Fred
who wants to borrow a rake.
Our sorry hound shifts in his hole,
surrenders to ninety-plus without a whimper.

We don't ask one question—
not about the mailman's ex
or why Fred needs a rake
in the hottest part of the day.
So hot, we sink into hammocks
and old vows of silence.
Soon enough evening will slide into place.

## At the Edge

Wait here at the edge
where anything can happen.
Don't lock the doors
or close the windows.
Unlatch your eyes and ears.
Open the cage of your heart
and let it breathe the way
it did when you were five.

Already the sun leaps
like a freed lion lunging
across the blue desert.
Do what he does.
Prowl the small forest.
Sniff the high grass;
roll in the low grass.
Lick the cheeks of those you love
and those you might love.
Follow his tango of quick paws
that advance, beat by beat,
to a grand finale of silence.
By evening, the old brute
will be tired, ready to slump
into the deep folds of night.

You'll be tired too
as the moon sails
with its fleet of stars.
Don't say no or maybe.
Growl if you need to.
Groom your paws.
So much happens
every minute.

# Last Night's Chicken Curry

Last night's chicken curry was a Nepali version
whose ancient aroma clung like fragrant vines
to every corner of our home.
Rafts of ardent spices floated
across the dull Western heartland of our kitchen.
Forget meatloaf and peas, jello and peaches.
Forget chicken breasts baked in cream.
Forget steamed fish and peeled potatoes.

Asian history and flavors transported us
to a cold mountain village where the smooth hands
of beautiful women, dark-haired in gracious saris,
stand like tall sultanas stirring sauce
and bubbly revolutions in shiny copper pots.
Crowded streets erupt in glossy golds and reds,
so much pushing and pulling, buying and selling.
Children and their pups run through muddy puddles;
white goats bleat and kick; impatient bearded men
on crimson pillows await their favorite curry.

Ours had morsels of chicken, threads of saffron,
golden cumin, fenugreek seeds, garum masala,
the amber soul of turmeric, plump garlic cloves diced
into white cubes of heat that clung to our palms,
sliced onions thin as damsel wings, topaz of ginger,
rough cardamom, and coriander leaves.
A perfect sauce, this Biblical creation.
Such a passion of eating, no grace could do it justice.

# Changing

Red-dusted leaves flicker
like clusters of small fires
crackling against a denim sky.
Early rains have turned
brown summer grass green,
each blade crowned with dew.

Days are bountiful with spiders
orb-stitching in every vacant arc;
in bare angles between post and rail
they've staked a plot of real estate
for themselves and progeny.
Even the porch broom propped
against the potting shelf tethers
a glistening web and in its center
an eight-legged guardian waits.

Our neighbor's horses, hidden
behind a blind of conifers,
stamp restless hooves and blow
nostril air to soothe themselves.
A deep quiet abides,
a deep breathing in and out—
time's at work, changing
gold to brown, warm to cold,
light to dark, leading us
to its kindly tent of rest.

# When the Power Goes Out

Fern fronds bend
at odd angles,
some flattened
by cushions of snow,
and the birdbath
wears a silver tray of ice,
in spots too thick to crack
with my cold finger.
Trees endure icy suits:
gaunt giants
with stiff, brittle arms.
Our driveway is snow packed
and slick, car doors sealed shut.
Yet here we are, oddly serene,
counting juncos at the suet.
Perhaps I've had a change
of heart about discomfort,
how it bends and consoles.

We have plenty of candles,
wool blankets,
pails of water in the kitchen,
and a bottle of red wine.
Most incredible is this quiet
that slips in like an old friend
who doesn't need to chat.
Our home is an ocean
of long shadows,
a kingdom of white peace.
Too soon, when the power
returns, this quiet world
will be erased.

# Local Weather

The weather man points to a wall-sized map
that's slightly out of focus—green smudges
of moderate calm shift north
beside a long orange curl of turbulence.
Wedged like slobs in front of the evening news,
we wait for today's unbearable truths.
Just give us something simple, mister,
like the low this morning or when the sun will set.
We can deal with that.

Dazed by the evening's jolt of crime,
we want to believe in something true as rain,
as if black hoods and body counts might, just might,
be washed away by evening showers.
It's hard to rise above our low-level doldrums
until we hear his weather blessing,
his final benediction that the coast is clear—
tonight and tomorrow too—then we haul our bodies
from the brink, fix dinner and a second drink,
consider if the next seven days will deliver
all he promised: sun, maybe evening showers,
no disaster in the forecast.
We won't hold him to it.

Later, submerged in friendly dark,
we turn to each other to confirm heat and cold,
grab a hand to hold.
Eventually a storm of one kind or another
will sweep away both good and evil.
Eternity alone has endless balmy weather:
winds calm, skies blue,
maybe light fog in the morning.

# The Bargain

Cold mornings don't stop him, not fog,
not rain that fingers down the neck of his yellow slicker.
This morning he digs potatoes
from mounds of damp, black dirt.
Then he twists ears of corn from tasseled stalks,
avoids intricate webs strung from husk to husk.
Small birds dive in and out, silent and intent.
Swallows skim Cinderella pumpkins
whose old-fashioned lamps glow orange and gold;
he takes a thick blade to hack their rugged stems.

The usual regrets erode his autumn mood of plenty—
beets left in the ground too long,
shriveled apples now wine mash for worms,
neglected seeds ordered months ago
nap in crowded packets.
Always the worry of too much to do
in the short time given.

After harvest, the season of decay—
that's a bargain he accepts,
the terms of this world we live in.

# Snowy Evening

Breaking trail through snow at dusk
from porch to hen house—
a big wolf moon pushing
close behind the Douglas firs—
I spot a great horned owl
above an alder snag.

Outlined against the soft lilac sky,
the great owl tips forward
on the verge of lifting into flight,
but no, he stretches his head and neck,
expands his chest,
and lets go an explosion of hoots
that shakes the silence beneath him.
When he does it again, another owl
in a farther snag calls back.

Although friends will arrive
any minute for omelets and wine,
I grab binoculars from the bench
and spend more time than I should
watching the moon and that bundle
of intent rise to the occasion
of this snowy evening.

# Celebration

It's not my favorite holiday.
Traffic gets worse each year,
and few of us are laughing all the way.
There's no river and no woods,
no horses or sleighs along Interstate-5.
If we brake in time, we might spot
that remnant patch of skinny trees
shivering behind the Wal-Mart parking lot.
Most Grandmas have moved
to a senior high rise or maybe to rehab.
Anyway, they're not baking pies.
The corpulent turkey, stripped
of its plastic jacket, shows no relation
to those wild bronze gobblers perched
in our imagination's forest.

The best part is now, home again
in our small corner of the woods.
Our cat is ecstatic that we've come back to her.
She charges down the stairs and slides around corners.
Like us, she thrills to smaller blessings:
that we return to fill her empty bowl,
that we descend from unexplored heights
to scratch her chin.

A cup of tea warms my palms.
You lift a glass of black-red wine
to toast owls crooning in the dark,
winter's low-slung moon,
our neighbor's bay mare
whose white wooly breath
hovers damp and hazy in the pasture.

# Three Deer

Mostly they come at half-light:
shudder of leaves at the forest edge,
shy reach of brown, then solid shapes
emerge from a fragrant stand of nine-bark and fir.
One week the larger male limped
far behind the others; he hasn't come again.

New homes mar these woods, consuming
browse and solitude: red-cheeked boys on bikes,
barbed wire fences that keep in, others that keep out.
Such landscapes don't account for deer.
I should have sent them scrambling at the start,
in their stiff-legged bolt, back to the silent woods
that bear no roads or country homes. Not yet.

Four months and still no sign, no tracks to count,
no broken boughs, just this—
October's fiery leaves raving on the ground,
repeated pops of hunters at their work,
Christmas rains confounding sodden earth.

New Year's Day we paused for resolutions
spiked with hope. But I have little hope.
They haven't crossed our land in months.

# When Santa Came to Town

Here's my vision of Christmas morning:
snow falling on every roof and tree, deep and still.
No gifts to divert us from the holy calm—
No trinkets from the mall.
No napkins stamped HoHoHo
or magnets for the fridge.

We'll have waffles and coffee,
brief news of the world outside
our white cocoon. With a second cup,
we'll sit by the fire, continue to praise
the weather—snowflakes proving
yet again the truth of time and change.

With minds unleashed from obligation,
thoughts will meander, as loose thoughts will,
to certain topics often neglected—death,
goodness, the unbearable happiness
we felt when we were young believers
and Santa came to town.

# Revelry

The family cat zipped in her plush black fur
snoozes near the fire, gently snoring,
committing every ounce
of her corporeal self to earthly comfort.
My husband on the sofa
inhales the heady fumes of Tolstoy's words.
He lowers his book to inform me
that Napoleon has taken Moscow
and winter's hard, blunt wheel has turned.
Then he looks away, eyes skidding
back to Russia's supreme snow.

Staying home with cat, book,
glass of wine is revelry enough.
We've had our share of celebrations
and disappointments too.
Out in the dark, cold world of time
cheerful revelers drink and dance;
midnight flares from zone to zone
until the sash of Earth fades
and the new year rises like a golden crown.

The cat stops snoring when I nudge her
with my toe. My husband keeps reading,
torn between New Year's Eve with me
and the glittering fireworks of Tolstoy.
Tonight he chooses Leo Nikolayevich.
So for this reveler a second glass of wine,
rich and red, and a toast to the old year,
a great doomed hulk that lists starboard
and sinks.

*Photograph by Greg Stone*

# About the Author

Diane Stone's work has been published in literary journals and anthologies such as *The Comstock Review, The Main Street Rag, Minerva Rising, Chautauqua,* and elsewhere. In 2015, she won the *Bacopa Literary Review* Poetry Prize. Born in Jacksonville, Florida, Diane retired after many years as a technical editor at a national research laboratory. She and her husband now live on Whidbey Island, north of Seattle, among five acres of forest, vegetable gardens, and native plants.

Kelsay Books

www.ingramcontent.com/pod-product-compliance
Lightning Source LLC
Chambersburg PA
CBHW071359090426
42738CB00012B/3168